50 Premium Ramen Restaurant Dishes

By: Kelly Johnson

Table of Contents

- Tonkotsu Ramen
- Shoyu Ramen
- Shio Ramen
- Miso Ramen
- Spicy Miso Ramen
- Tsukemen (Dipping Ramen)
- Hakata Tonkotsu Ramen
- Hokkaido Miso Ramen
- Yaki Ramen (Fried Ramen)
- Ramen Burger
- Black Garlic Tonkotsu Ramen
- Kimchi Ramen
- Chili Oil Ramen
- Tantanmen (Spicy Sesame Ramen)
- Crab Ramen
- Truffle Ramen
- Curry Ramen
- Ramen with Char Siu Pork
- Ramen with Braised Beef
- Ramen with Fish Cake
- Ramen with Soft-Boiled Egg
- Chicken Ramen
- Prawn Ramen
- Vegan Ramen
- Vegetarian Miso Ramen
- Hiyashi Chuka (Cold Ramen)
- Tonkotsu-Shoyu Ramen
- Beef Sukiyaki Ramen
- Sapporo Ramen
- Abura Soba (Oil Ramen)
- Gyoza Ramen
- Kimchi Spicy Ramen
- Soy Milk Ramen
- Ramen with Seaweed
- Spicy Tuna Ramen
- Spicy Garlic Ramen

- Paitan Ramen (Rich Chicken Broth)
- Udon Ramen Fusion
- Ramen with Tempura
- Mentaiko Ramen (Spicy Cod Roe)
- Ramen with Sweet Corn
- Ramen with Tofu
- Ramen with Pork Belly
- Shoyu Tsukemen
- Chashu Ramen
- Ramen with Bamboo Shoots
- Ramen with Black Bean Paste
- Lobster Ramen
- Ramen with Truffle Oil
- Ramen with Soft Shell Crab

Tonkotsu Ramen

Ingredients:

- 4 cups pork bone broth (or chicken stock if unavailable)
- 1 tablespoon sesame oil
- 1 tablespoon soy sauce
- 2 teaspoons mirin
- 4 ramen noodles
- 2 boiled eggs, soft-boiled
- 1/2 cup sliced pork belly or chashu
- 1/2 cup chopped green onions
- 1 sheet nori (seaweed)
- 1 tablespoon garlic, minced
- 1 tablespoon ginger, minced

Instructions:

1. In a large pot, combine the pork bone broth, sesame oil, soy sauce, and mirin. Bring to a simmer.
2. In a separate pot, cook the ramen noodles according to package instructions, then drain and set aside.
3. In a small pan, sauté garlic and ginger in a bit of oil until fragrant. Add to the broth mixture.
4. Add the cooked noodles to the soup and let them soak in the broth for 1-2 minutes.
5. Top with sliced pork belly, soft-boiled eggs, chopped green onions, and nori. Serve hot.

Shoyu Ramen

Ingredients:

- 4 cups chicken or pork broth
- 1/4 cup soy sauce
- 1 tablespoon mirin
- 1 tablespoon rice vinegar
- 4 ramen noodles
- 2 boiled eggs, soft-boiled
- 1/2 cup sliced chashu (braised pork belly)
- 1/2 cup green onions, chopped
- 1 tablespoon sesame oil
- 1/2 teaspoon dried seaweed (optional)

Instructions:

1. Bring the chicken or pork broth to a simmer in a large pot.
2. Stir in soy sauce, mirin, rice vinegar, and sesame oil. Let simmer for 10 minutes to develop flavors.
3. Cook the ramen noodles according to package instructions, drain, and place in bowls.
4. Pour the broth over the noodles.
5. Top with chashu, soft-boiled eggs, green onions, and a sprinkle of seaweed.

Shio Ramen

Ingredients:

- 4 cups chicken or pork broth
- 1 tablespoon salt (adjust to taste)
- 1 tablespoon soy sauce
- 1 tablespoon sake
- 4 ramen noodles
- 2 boiled eggs, soft-boiled
- 1/2 cup sliced chicken or chashu
- 1/4 cup bamboo shoots, sliced
- 1/4 cup green onions, chopped

Instructions:

1. In a pot, bring chicken or pork broth to a simmer.
2. Add salt, soy sauce, and sake. Taste and adjust seasoning.
3. Cook the ramen noodles according to package instructions.
4. Serve noodles in bowls, pour the broth over them, and top with chicken, soft-boiled eggs, bamboo shoots, and green onions.

Miso Ramen

Ingredients:

- 4 cups chicken or vegetable broth
- 3 tablespoons miso paste (white or red)
- 1 tablespoon sesame oil
- 1 tablespoon soy sauce
- 1 tablespoon mirin
- 4 ramen noodles
- 2 boiled eggs, soft-boiled
- 1/2 cup sliced pork or tofu
- 1/4 cup green onions, chopped
- 1/4 cup corn (optional)
- 1 sheet nori (optional)

Instructions:

1. In a pot, heat sesame oil over medium heat. Add miso paste and sauté for 1-2 minutes.
2. Add chicken or vegetable broth, soy sauce, and mirin. Simmer for 10 minutes.
3. Cook ramen noodles according to package instructions.
4. Place noodles in bowls, pour broth over them.
5. Top with sliced pork or tofu, soft-boiled eggs, corn, green onions, and nori.

Spicy Miso Ramen

Ingredients:

- 4 cups chicken or vegetable broth
- 3 tablespoons miso paste
- 1 tablespoon sesame oil
- 1 tablespoon soy sauce
- 1 tablespoon chili paste or gochujang (for heat)
- 4 ramen noodles
- 2 boiled eggs, soft-boiled
- 1/2 cup sliced pork or tofu
- 1/4 cup chopped green onions
- 1/4 cup bamboo shoots

Instructions:

1. Heat sesame oil in a pot, then add miso paste and chili paste. Sauté for 1-2 minutes.
2. Add broth, soy sauce, and bring to a simmer.
3. Cook ramen noodles, then place in bowls.
4. Pour broth over the noodles, and top with pork or tofu, soft-boiled eggs, green onions, and bamboo shoots.

Tsukemen (Dipping Ramen)

Ingredients:

- 4 cups chicken or pork broth (for dipping)
- 2 tablespoons soy sauce
- 1 tablespoon sesame oil
- 1 tablespoon mirin
- 4 ramen noodles
- 1/2 cup sliced chashu or chicken
- 2 boiled eggs, soft-boiled
- 1/4 cup bamboo shoots, sliced
- 1/4 cup green onions, chopped
- 1 tablespoon toasted sesame seeds

Instructions:

1. In a pot, bring the broth to a simmer, then add soy sauce, sesame oil, and mirin. Let it simmer for 10 minutes.
2. Cook the ramen noodles according to package instructions, then rinse under cold water to stop cooking.
3. Serve the noodles on a separate plate or bowl with dipping broth on the side.
4. Top with chashu, soft-boiled eggs, bamboo shoots, green onions, and sesame seeds.
5. To eat, dip the noodles into the broth before slurping.

Hakata Tonkotsu Ramen

Ingredients:

- 4 cups pork bone broth
- 2 tablespoons soy sauce
- 1 tablespoon sesame oil
- 1 tablespoon mirin
- 4 ramen noodles (thin)
- 2 boiled eggs, soft-boiled
- 1/2 cup chashu (braised pork belly)
- 1/4 cup green onions, chopped
- 1 sheet nori

Instructions:

1. In a large pot, bring pork bone broth to a simmer and stir in soy sauce, sesame oil, and mirin.
2. Cook ramen noodles according to package instructions.
3. Add noodles to bowls and pour the broth over.
4. Top with chashu, soft-boiled eggs, green onions, and nori.

Hokkaido Miso Ramen

Ingredients:

- 4 cups chicken or vegetable broth
- 2 tablespoons miso paste
- 1 tablespoon sesame oil
- 1 tablespoon soy sauce
- 1 tablespoon mirin
- 4 ramen noodles
- 2 boiled eggs, soft-boiled
- 1/2 cup corn kernels
- 1/2 cup sliced pork or tofu
- 1/4 cup green onions

Instructions:

1. In a pot, heat sesame oil and sauté miso paste for 2-3 minutes.
2. Add broth, soy sauce, and mirin, then bring to a simmer.
3. Cook the noodles according to package instructions.
4. Add noodles to bowls, pour broth over, and top with corn, pork or tofu, soft-boiled eggs, and green onions.

Yaki Ramen (Fried Ramen)

Ingredients:

- 4 ramen noodles
- 1 tablespoon sesame oil
- 1/2 cup sliced mushrooms
- 1/2 cup sliced bell peppers
- 1/2 cup shredded cabbage
- 1/4 cup soy sauce
- 1 tablespoon oyster sauce
- 1 tablespoon sugar
- 1 teaspoon garlic powder
- 2 boiled eggs, soft-boiled
- Green onions for garnish

Instructions:

1. Cook ramen noodles according to package instructions, then drain and set aside.
2. In a large pan or wok, heat sesame oil over medium-high heat.
3. Add mushrooms, bell peppers, and cabbage. Stir-fry for 2-3 minutes.
4. Add noodles to the pan, then mix in soy sauce, oyster sauce, sugar, and garlic powder.
5. Fry for 2-3 minutes until noodles are slightly crispy.
6. Serve with soft-boiled eggs and green onions.

Ramen Burger

Ingredients:

- 2 packs of instant ramen noodles (discard the seasoning)
- 1 tablespoon soy sauce
- 2 hamburger buns
- 1/2 lb ground beef
- 1/4 cup shredded lettuce
- 1/4 cup sliced tomatoes
- 2 slices American cheese
- 1 tablespoon mayonnaise

Instructions:

1. Cook the ramen noodles, then drain and let cool slightly. Mix with soy sauce and form into two patties.
2. In a skillet, cook the ramen patties over medium heat for 2-3 minutes on each side until crispy.
3. Cook the ground beef into two burger patties, seasoning with salt and pepper.
4. Toast the buns in the same skillet.
5. Assemble the burger: place a ramen patty on each bun, top with beef patty, cheese, lettuce, tomato, and mayonnaise.

Black Garlic Tonkotsu Ramen

Ingredients:

- 4 cups pork bone broth
- 2 tablespoons black garlic oil
- 1 tablespoon soy sauce
- 1 tablespoon sesame oil
- 4 ramen noodles
- 1/2 cup sliced chashu or pork belly
- 2 boiled eggs, soft-boiled
- 1/4 cup green onions, chopped
- 1 sheet nori

Instructions:

1. In a pot, bring the pork bone broth to a simmer and stir in soy sauce, black garlic oil, and sesame oil.
2. Cook ramen noodles according to package instructions.
3. Place noodles in bowls and pour the broth over them.
4. Top with chashu, soft-boiled eggs, green onions, and nori.

Kimchi Ramen

Ingredients:

- 4 cups chicken or vegetable broth
- 1/2 cup kimchi, chopped
- 1 tablespoon soy sauce
- 1 tablespoon gochujang (Korean chili paste)
- 4 ramen noodles
- 1/2 cup sliced pork belly or tofu
- 1/4 cup green onions, chopped
- 1 boiled egg, soft-boiled

Instructions:

1. In a pot, combine the chicken or vegetable broth, kimchi, soy sauce, and gochujang. Bring to a simmer.
2. Cook the ramen noodles according to package instructions.
3. Add the cooked noodles to the broth, simmering for 1-2 minutes.
4. Top with sliced pork belly or tofu, soft-boiled egg, and green onions.

Chili Oil Ramen

Ingredients:

- 4 cups chicken or pork broth
- 2 tablespoons chili oil
- 1 tablespoon soy sauce
- 1 tablespoon sesame oil
- 4 ramen noodles
- 1/2 cup sliced chicken or beef
- 1/4 cup green onions, chopped
- 1 tablespoon garlic, minced

Instructions:

1. Heat sesame oil in a pot, add minced garlic, and cook until fragrant.
2. Add chicken or pork broth, soy sauce, and chili oil. Bring to a simmer.
3. Cook the ramen noodles according to package instructions.
4. Place the noodles in bowls, pour the broth over them, and top with sliced chicken or beef and green onions.

Tantanmen (Spicy Sesame Ramen)

Ingredients:

- 4 cups chicken or vegetable broth
- 2 tablespoons tahini or sesame paste
- 1 tablespoon soy sauce
- 1 tablespoon chili paste or paste (optional for heat)
- 4 ramen noodles
- 1/2 cup ground pork or chicken
- 1 tablespoon sesame oil
- 1 boiled egg, soft-boiled
- 1/4 cup green onions, chopped
- 1 tablespoon crushed peanuts (optional)

Instructions:

1. In a pot, heat sesame oil and cook ground pork or chicken until browned.
2. Add the broth, tahini, soy sauce, and chili paste (optional). Bring to a simmer.
3. Cook the ramen noodles according to package instructions.
4. Place noodles in bowls, pour the broth over, and top with the cooked meat, soft-boiled egg, green onions, and crushed peanuts.

Crab Ramen

Ingredients:

- 4 cups seafood broth or chicken broth
- 1/2 cup crab meat (fresh or canned)
- 1 tablespoon soy sauce
- 1 tablespoon sesame oil
- 4 ramen noodles
- 1/2 cup sliced mushrooms
- 1/4 cup green onions, chopped
- 1 boiled egg, soft-boiled

Instructions:

1. In a pot, bring the seafood broth to a simmer. Add soy sauce and sesame oil.
2. Add the crab meat and mushrooms to the broth and cook for a few minutes.
3. Cook the ramen noodles according to package instructions.
4. Place noodles in bowls, pour the broth over, and top with crab meat, soft-boiled egg, and green onions.

Truffle Ramen

Ingredients:

- 4 cups chicken or vegetable broth
- 1 tablespoon truffle oil (or truffle paste)
- 4 ramen noodles
- 1/2 cup sliced shiitake mushrooms
- 1 boiled egg, soft-boiled
- 1/4 cup parmesan cheese, grated
- 1 tablespoon soy sauce
- Fresh parsley, chopped (for garnish)

Instructions:

1. In a pot, bring the chicken or vegetable broth to a simmer.
2. Add soy sauce and truffle oil to the broth, then add the shiitake mushrooms. Simmer for a few minutes.
3. Cook the ramen noodles according to package instructions.
4. Place noodles in bowls, pour the broth over, and top with soft-boiled egg, parmesan cheese, and parsley.

Curry Ramen

Ingredients:

- 4 cups chicken or vegetable broth
- 2 tablespoons curry paste or curry powder
- 1 tablespoon soy sauce
- 1 tablespoon sesame oil
- 4 ramen noodles
- 1/2 cup sliced chicken or beef
- 1 boiled egg, soft-boiled
- 1/4 cup green onions, chopped

Instructions:

1. In a pot, heat sesame oil and sauté the curry paste or curry powder until fragrant.
2. Add chicken or vegetable broth and soy sauce. Bring to a simmer.
3. Cook the ramen noodles according to package instructions.
4. Place noodles in bowls, pour the curry broth over, and top with sliced chicken or beef, soft-boiled egg, and green onions.

Ramen with Char Siu Pork

Ingredients:

- 4 cups chicken broth
- 1/2 cup Char Siu pork (Chinese BBQ pork), sliced
- 1 tablespoon soy sauce
- 1 tablespoon sesame oil
- 4 ramen noodles
- 1 boiled egg, soft-boiled
- 1/4 cup green onions, chopped

Instructions:

1. Heat the chicken broth in a pot and stir in soy sauce and sesame oil. Bring to a simmer.
2. Cook the ramen noodles according to package instructions.
3. Place noodles in bowls, pour the broth over, and top with Char Siu pork, soft-boiled egg, and green onions.

Ramen with Braised Beef

Ingredients:

- 4 cups beef broth
- 1/2 cup braised beef (prepared beforehand)
- 1 tablespoon soy sauce
- 1 tablespoon sesame oil
- 4 ramen noodles
- 1 boiled egg, soft-boiled
- 1/4 cup green onions, chopped

Instructions:

1. Heat the beef broth in a pot and stir in soy sauce and sesame oil. Bring to a simmer.
2. Cook the ramen noodles according to package instructions.
3. Place noodles in bowls, pour the broth over, and top with braised beef, soft-boiled egg, and green onions.

Ramen with Fish Cake

Ingredients:

- 4 cups chicken broth
- 2 fish cakes (narutomaki), sliced
- 1 tablespoon soy sauce
- 1 tablespoon sesame oil
- 4 ramen noodles
- 1 boiled egg, soft-boiled
- 1/4 cup green onions, chopped

Instructions:

1. In a pot, bring the chicken broth to a simmer and stir in soy sauce and sesame oil.
2. Cook the ramen noodles according to package instructions.
3. Place noodles in bowls, pour the broth over, and top with fish cakes, soft-boiled egg, and green onions.

Ramen with Soft-Boiled Egg

Ingredients:

- 4 cups chicken or vegetable broth
- 1 tablespoon soy sauce
- 1 tablespoon sesame oil
- 4 ramen noodles
- 2 soft-boiled eggs
- 1/4 cup green onions, chopped

Instructions:

1. In a pot, bring the broth to a simmer and add soy sauce and sesame oil.
2. Cook the ramen noodles according to package instructions.
3. Place noodles in bowls, pour the broth over, and top with soft-boiled eggs and green onions.

Chicken Ramen

Ingredients:

- 4 cups chicken broth
- 2 tablespoons soy sauce
- 1 tablespoon sesame oil
- 4 ramen noodles
- 1/2 cup sliced chicken breast or thigh
- 1 boiled egg, soft-boiled
- 1/4 cup green onions, chopped
- 1/4 cup bamboo shoots, sliced

Instructions:

1. In a pot, bring the chicken broth to a simmer. Add soy sauce and sesame oil.
2. Cook the ramen noodles according to package instructions.
3. Place noodles in bowls, pour the broth over them, and top with sliced chicken, soft-boiled egg, green onions, and bamboo shoots.

Prawn Ramen

Ingredients:

- 4 cups seafood or chicken broth
- 1/2 pound prawns, peeled and deveined
- 2 tablespoons soy sauce
- 1 tablespoon sesame oil
- 4 ramen noodles
- 1 boiled egg, soft-boiled
- 1/4 cup green onions, chopped
- 1/4 cup sliced mushrooms

Instructions:

1. In a pot, bring the broth to a simmer. Add soy sauce and sesame oil.
2. Add prawns and cook for 2-3 minutes until pink.
3. Cook the ramen noodles according to package instructions.
4. Place noodles in bowls, pour the broth and prawns over, and top with soft-boiled egg, green onions, and mushrooms.

Vegan Ramen

Ingredients:

- 4 cups vegetable broth
- 1 tablespoon soy sauce
- 1 tablespoon sesame oil
- 4 ramen noodles
- 1/2 cup tofu, cubed
- 1/4 cup sliced mushrooms
- 1/4 cup spinach or bok choy
- 1 boiled egg (optional, for non-vegan version)
- 1/4 cup green onions, chopped

Instructions:

1. In a pot, bring the vegetable broth to a simmer and stir in soy sauce and sesame oil.
2. Add tofu, mushrooms, and spinach. Cook for a few minutes until the vegetables are tender.
3. Cook the ramen noodles according to package instructions.
4. Place noodles in bowls, pour the broth and vegetables over, and top with tofu, soft-boiled egg (if desired), and green onions.

Vegetarian Miso Ramen

Ingredients:

- 4 cups vegetable broth
- 2 tablespoons miso paste
- 1 tablespoon soy sauce
- 1 tablespoon sesame oil
- 4 ramen noodles
- 1/2 cup tofu or tempeh, cubed
- 1/4 cup sliced mushrooms
- 1 boiled egg (optional, for non-vegan version)
- 1/4 cup green onions, chopped

Instructions:

1. In a pot, bring the vegetable broth to a simmer and add miso paste, soy sauce, and sesame oil.
2. Add tofu and mushrooms, and cook until heated through.
3. Cook the ramen noodles according to package instructions.
4. Place noodles in bowls, pour the broth over, and top with tofu, soft-boiled egg (if desired), and green onions.

Hiyashi Chuka (Cold Ramen)

Ingredients:

- 4 cups chicken or vegetable broth
- 1 tablespoon soy sauce
- 1 tablespoon rice vinegar
- 1 tablespoon sesame oil
- 4 ramen noodles (chilled)
- 1/4 cup cucumber, julienned
- 1/4 cup carrots, julienned
- 1 boiled egg, sliced
- 1/4 cup cooked chicken or tofu
- 1 tablespoon sesame seeds
- 1/4 cup green onions, chopped

Instructions:

1. Cook the ramen noodles according to package instructions, rinse under cold water, and set aside.
2. In a bowl, mix soy sauce, rice vinegar, sesame oil, and a splash of broth to make a dressing.
3. Arrange the cold noodles in a bowl. Top with cucumber, carrots, sliced egg, chicken or tofu, sesame seeds, and green onions.
4. Drizzle the dressing over the noodles and serve chilled.

Tonkotsu-Shoyu Ramen

Ingredients:

- 4 cups pork bone broth
- 2 tablespoons soy sauce
- 1 tablespoon sesame oil
- 4 ramen noodles
- 1/2 cup sliced chashu (braised pork belly)
- 1 boiled egg, soft-boiled
- 1/4 cup green onions, chopped
- 1/2 cup bamboo shoots, sliced

Instructions:

1. In a pot, bring the pork bone broth to a simmer and stir in soy sauce and sesame oil.
2. Cook the ramen noodles according to package instructions.
3. Place noodles in bowls, pour the broth over them, and top with chashu, soft-boiled egg, green onions, and bamboo shoots.

Beef Sukiyaki Ramen

Ingredients:

- 4 cups beef broth
- 1/2 cup thinly sliced beef (sukiyaki-style)
- 2 tablespoons soy sauce
- 1 tablespoon mirin
- 4 ramen noodles
- 1/4 cup shiitake mushrooms, sliced
- 1 boiled egg, soft-boiled
- 1/4 cup green onions, chopped

Instructions:

1. In a pot, bring beef broth to a simmer. Add soy sauce, mirin, and sliced beef. Cook the beef until tender.
2. Cook the ramen noodles according to package instructions.
3. Place noodles in bowls, pour the broth and beef over, and top with shiitake mushrooms, soft-boiled egg, and green onions.

Sapporo Ramen

Ingredients:

- 4 cups chicken or pork broth
- 2 tablespoons miso paste
- 1 tablespoon soy sauce
- 1 tablespoon sesame oil
- 4 ramen noodles
- 1/2 cup corn kernels
- 1/2 cup sliced chashu pork
- 1 boiled egg, soft-boiled
- 1/4 cup green onions, chopped

Instructions:

1. In a pot, heat sesame oil and stir in miso paste, soy sauce, and broth. Bring to a simmer.
2. Add corn and cook for a few minutes.
3. Cook the ramen noodles according to package instructions.
4. Place noodles in bowls, pour the broth over them, and top with chashu pork, soft-boiled egg, and green onions.

Abura Soba (Oil Ramen)

Ingredients:

- 4 cups chicken or vegetable broth
- 2 tablespoons soy sauce
- 1 tablespoon sesame oil
- 4 ramen noodles
- 1 tablespoon chili oil (optional for spice)
- 1/4 cup green onions, chopped
- 1 boiled egg, soft-boiled
- 1/2 cup cooked chicken or pork

Instructions:

1. Cook the ramen noodles according to package instructions, then drain and set aside.
2. In a bowl, mix soy sauce, sesame oil, and chili oil (optional).
3. Toss the cooked noodles in the oil mixture.
4. Serve with cooked chicken or pork, soft-boiled egg, and green onions.

Gyoza Ramen

Ingredients:

- 4 cups chicken or vegetable broth
- 1 tablespoon soy sauce
- 1 tablespoon sesame oil
- 4 ramen noodles
- 4-6 gyoza (Japanese dumplings), steamed or fried
- 1/4 cup green onions, chopped
- 1 boiled egg, soft-boiled

Instructions:

1. In a pot, bring the broth to a simmer and add soy sauce and sesame oil.
2. Cook the ramen noodles according to package instructions.
3. Place noodles in bowls, pour the broth over, and top with gyoza, soft-boiled egg, and green onions.

Kimchi Spicy Ramen

Ingredients:

- 4 cups chicken or vegetable broth
- 1/2 cup kimchi, chopped
- 1 tablespoon gochujang (Korean chili paste)
- 4 ramen noodles
- 1/4 cup sliced pork belly or tofu
- 1 tablespoon sesame oil
- 1 boiled egg, soft-boiled
- 1/4 cup green onions, chopped

Instructions:

1. In a pot, combine the chicken or vegetable broth, kimchi, gochujang, and sesame oil. Bring to a simmer.
2. Cook the ramen noodles according to package instructions.
3. Add the cooked noodles to the broth, simmer for 1-2 minutes.
4. Top with sliced pork belly or tofu, soft-boiled egg, and green onions.

Soy Milk Ramen

Ingredients:

- 4 cups vegetable broth
- 1 cup unsweetened soy milk
- 1 tablespoon soy sauce
- 1 tablespoon sesame oil
- 4 ramen noodles
- 1/2 cup mushrooms, sliced
- 1 boiled egg, soft-boiled
- 1/4 cup green onions, chopped
- 1 tablespoon sesame seeds

Instructions:

1. In a pot, combine vegetable broth and soy milk. Bring to a simmer.
2. Add soy sauce, sesame oil, and mushrooms, and cook for 3-4 minutes.
3. Cook the ramen noodles according to package instructions.
4. Place noodles in bowls, pour the soy milk broth over, and top with soft-boiled egg, green onions, and sesame seeds.

Ramen with Seaweed

Ingredients:

- 4 cups chicken or vegetable broth
- 1 tablespoon soy sauce
- 1 tablespoon sesame oil
- 4 ramen noodles
- 1/2 cup nori or wakame seaweed (dried or rehydrated)
- 1 boiled egg, soft-boiled
- 1/4 cup green onions, chopped
- 1 tablespoon sesame seeds

Instructions:

1. In a pot, bring the chicken or vegetable broth to a simmer and add soy sauce and sesame oil.
2. Cook the ramen noodles according to package instructions.
3. Place noodles in bowls, pour the broth over, and top with seaweed, soft-boiled egg, green onions, and sesame seeds.

Spicy Tuna Ramen

Ingredients:

- 4 cups chicken or vegetable broth
- 1 tablespoon sriracha or chili paste
- 4 ramen noodles
- 1/2 cup canned tuna, drained
- 1 tablespoon sesame oil
- 1 boiled egg, soft-boiled
- 1/4 cup green onions, chopped

Instructions:

1. In a pot, combine the chicken or vegetable broth with sriracha or chili paste and sesame oil. Bring to a simmer.
2. Cook the ramen noodles according to package instructions.
3. Place noodles in bowls, pour the spicy broth over, and top with tuna, soft-boiled egg, and green onions.

Spicy Garlic Ramen

Ingredients:

- 4 cups chicken or vegetable broth
- 1 tablespoon chili oil
- 3-4 cloves garlic, minced
- 4 ramen noodles
- 1 tablespoon soy sauce
- 1 boiled egg, soft-boiled
- 1/4 cup green onions, chopped
- 1 tablespoon sesame seeds

Instructions:

1. In a pot, heat chili oil and sauté the minced garlic until fragrant.
2. Add chicken or vegetable broth and soy sauce, then bring to a simmer.
3. Cook the ramen noodles according to package instructions.
4. Place noodles in bowls, pour the spicy garlic broth over, and top with soft-boiled egg, green onions, and sesame seeds.

Paitan Ramen (Rich Chicken Broth)

Ingredients:

- 4 cups chicken broth (preferably from boiling chicken bones for several hours)
- 2 tablespoons soy sauce
- 1 tablespoon sesame oil
- 4 ramen noodles
- 1/2 cup sliced chicken breast or thigh
- 1 boiled egg, soft-boiled
- 1/4 cup green onions, chopped

Instructions:

1. In a pot, bring the rich chicken broth to a simmer and stir in soy sauce and sesame oil.
2. Cook the ramen noodles according to package instructions.
3. Place noodles in bowls, pour the paitan broth over, and top with sliced chicken, soft-boiled egg, and green onions.

Udon Ramen Fusion

Ingredients:

- 4 cups chicken or vegetable broth
- 1 tablespoon soy sauce
- 1 tablespoon sesame oil
- 4 ramen noodles (or udon noodles for a fusion twist)
- 1/2 cup shiitake mushrooms, sliced
- 1 boiled egg, soft-boiled
- 1/4 cup green onions, chopped

Instructions:

1. In a pot, bring the chicken or vegetable broth to a simmer and stir in soy sauce and sesame oil.
2. Cook the udon or ramen noodles according to package instructions.
3. Place noodles in bowls, pour the broth over, and top with shiitake mushrooms, soft-boiled egg, and green onions.

Ramen with Tempura

Ingredients:

- 4 cups chicken or vegetable broth
- 1 tablespoon soy sauce
- 1 tablespoon sesame oil
- 4 ramen noodles
- 2-3 pieces of tempura (shrimp or vegetable)
- 1 boiled egg, soft-boiled
- 1/4 cup green onions, chopped

Instructions:

1. In a pot, bring the chicken or vegetable broth to a simmer and stir in soy sauce and sesame oil.
2. Cook the ramen noodles according to package instructions.
3. Place noodles in bowls, pour the broth over, and top with tempura, soft-boiled egg, and green onions.

Mentaiko Ramen (Spicy Cod Roe)

Ingredients:

- 4 cups chicken or vegetable broth
- 2 tablespoons mentaiko (spicy cod roe), roughly mashed
- 1 tablespoon soy sauce
- 1 tablespoon sesame oil
- 4 ramen noodles
- 1 boiled egg, soft-boiled
- 1/4 cup green onions, chopped

Instructions:

1. In a pot, bring the chicken or vegetable broth to a simmer and stir in soy sauce, sesame oil, and mentaiko.
2. Cook the ramen noodles according to package instructions.
3. Place noodles in bowls, pour the mentaiko broth over, and top with soft-boiled egg and green onions.

Ramen with Sweet Corn

Ingredients:

- 4 cups chicken or vegetable broth
- 1 tablespoon soy sauce
- 1 tablespoon sesame oil
- 4 ramen noodles
- 1/2 cup corn kernels (fresh or frozen)
- 1 boiled egg, soft-boiled
- 1/4 cup green onions, chopped

Instructions:

1. In a pot, bring the chicken or vegetable broth to a simmer and stir in soy sauce and sesame oil.
2. Add corn kernels and cook for a few minutes until heated through.
3. Cook the ramen noodles according to package instructions.
4. Place noodles in bowls, pour the broth and corn over, and top with soft-boiled egg and green onions.

Ramen with Tofu

Ingredients:

- 4 cups vegetable broth
- 1 tablespoon soy sauce
- 1 tablespoon sesame oil
- 4 ramen noodles
- 1/2 cup tofu, cubed
- 1/4 cup spinach or bok choy
- 1 boiled egg, soft-boiled
- 1/4 cup green onions, chopped
- 1 tablespoon sesame seeds

Instructions:

1. In a pot, bring the vegetable broth to a simmer, and stir in soy sauce and sesame oil.
2. Add tofu and spinach, cooking until the spinach is wilted.
3. Cook the ramen noodles according to package instructions.
4. Place noodles in bowls, pour the broth over, and top with tofu, soft-boiled egg, green onions, and sesame seeds.

Ramen with Pork Belly

Ingredients:

- 4 cups chicken or pork broth
- 1 tablespoon soy sauce
- 1 tablespoon sesame oil
- 4 ramen noodles
- 1/2 cup sliced pork belly (braised or roasted)
- 1 boiled egg, soft-boiled
- 1/4 cup green onions, chopped
- 1/4 cup bamboo shoots, sliced

Instructions:

1. In a pot, bring the chicken or pork broth to a simmer, and stir in soy sauce and sesame oil.
2. Cook the ramen noodles according to package instructions.
3. Place noodles in bowls, pour the broth over, and top with sliced pork belly, soft-boiled egg, green onions, and bamboo shoots.

Shoyu Tsukemen (Dipping Ramen)

Ingredients:

- 4 cups chicken or vegetable broth
- 2 tablespoons soy sauce
- 1 tablespoon sesame oil
- 4 ramen noodles
- 1/4 cup sliced pork belly (optional)
- 1/4 cup green onions, chopped
- 1 boiled egg, soft-boiled

Instructions:

1. In a pot, bring the chicken or vegetable broth to a simmer and stir in soy sauce and sesame oil.
2. Cook the ramen noodles according to package instructions. Drain and set aside.
3. Serve the noodles separately in a bowl, with the dipping broth alongside in another bowl.
4. Top the broth with sliced pork belly (optional), green onions, and soft-boiled egg.
5. Dip the noodles into the broth before eating.

Chashu Ramen

Ingredients:

- 4 cups pork broth
- 2 tablespoons soy sauce
- 1 tablespoon sesame oil
- 4 ramen noodles
- 1/2 cup chashu pork (braised pork belly), thinly sliced
- 1 boiled egg, soft-boiled
- 1/4 cup green onions, chopped
- 1/4 cup bamboo shoots, sliced

Instructions:

1. In a pot, bring the pork broth to a simmer, and stir in soy sauce and sesame oil.
2. Cook the ramen noodles according to package instructions.
3. Place noodles in bowls, pour the broth over, and top with chashu pork, soft-boiled egg, green onions, and bamboo shoots.

Ramen with Bamboo Shoots

Ingredients:

- 4 cups chicken or vegetable broth
- 1 tablespoon soy sauce
- 1 tablespoon sesame oil
- 4 ramen noodles
- 1/2 cup bamboo shoots, sliced
- 1 boiled egg, soft-boiled
- 1/4 cup green onions, chopped

Instructions:

1. In a pot, bring the chicken or vegetable broth to a simmer, and stir in soy sauce and sesame oil.
2. Add bamboo shoots and cook for 2-3 minutes.
3. Cook the ramen noodles according to package instructions.
4. Place noodles in bowls, pour the broth over, and top with bamboo shoots, soft-boiled egg, and green onions.

Ramen with Black Bean Paste

Ingredients:

- 4 cups vegetable broth
- 2 tablespoons black bean paste (chunjang)
- 1 tablespoon soy sauce
- 4 ramen noodles
- 1 boiled egg, soft-boiled
- 1/4 cup green onions, chopped
- 1 tablespoon sesame oil

Instructions:

1. In a pot, heat sesame oil and stir in black bean paste until fragrant.
2. Add vegetable broth and soy sauce. Bring to a simmer.
3. Cook the ramen noodles according to package instructions.
4. Place noodles in bowls, pour the broth over, and top with soft-boiled egg and green onions.

Lobster Ramen

Ingredients:

- 4 cups seafood broth
- 1 lobster tail, peeled and chopped
- 1 tablespoon soy sauce
- 1 tablespoon sesame oil
- 4 ramen noodles
- 1/4 cup green onions, chopped
- 1 boiled egg, soft-boiled

Instructions:

1. In a pot, bring the seafood broth to a simmer and stir in soy sauce and sesame oil.
2. Add lobster meat and cook for 2-3 minutes.
3. Cook the ramen noodles according to package instructions.
4. Place noodles in bowls, pour the broth and lobster over, and top with soft-boiled egg and green onions.

Ramen with Truffle Oil

Ingredients:

- 4 cups chicken or vegetable broth
- 1 tablespoon soy sauce
- 1 tablespoon sesame oil
- 4 ramen noodles
- 1 tablespoon truffle oil
- 1 boiled egg, soft-boiled
- 1/4 cup green onions, chopped
- 1 tablespoon grated Parmesan cheese (optional)

Instructions:

1. In a pot, bring the chicken or vegetable broth to a simmer and stir in soy sauce and sesame oil.
2. Cook the ramen noodles according to package instructions.
3. Drizzle truffle oil over the cooked noodles before serving.
4. Top with soft-boiled egg, green onions, and Parmesan cheese (if desired).

Ramen with Soft Shell Crab

Ingredients:

- 4 cups seafood broth
- 1-2 soft shell crabs (fried)
- 1 tablespoon soy sauce
- 1 tablespoon sesame oil
- 4 ramen noodles
- 1 boiled egg, soft-boiled
- 1/4 cup green onions, chopped

Instructions:

1. In a pot, bring the seafood broth to a simmer and stir in soy sauce and sesame oil.
2. Cook the ramen noodles according to package instructions.
3. Place noodles in bowls, pour the broth over, and top with fried soft shell crab, soft-boiled egg, and green onions.

www.ingramcontent.com/pod-product-compliance
Lightning Source LLC
LaVergne TN
LVHW081501060526
838201LV00056BA/2861